listen to the music and watch the video as you color

Author Robert Schmidt

Performed by Joe Calautti

ISBN 979-8-89428-269-5 (paperback)
ISBN 979-8-89428-270-1 (digital)

Christian Faith Publishing
832 Park Avenue
Meadville, PA 16335
www.christianfaithpublishing.com

Printed in the United States of America

I love the father and the father loves me

He loves everything from the sky to the sea

He sent his only son to save me

So we could live in heaven for eternity

Thank you God
for sending Jesus as my savior

The Son the Father and the Holy Ghost

These are the things in life I love the most

Nothing in this world will last for long

For ever up in Heaven is where we belong

Thank You God
for sending Jesus as my savior
10

11

peace joy harmony and all the best

There I shall not worry there i shall not cry
13

The Lord has made a home for us up in the sky

Thank You God
I
JESUS
for sending Jesus as my savior
15

Draw your own picture of Heaven
and color

Draw a picture of your family and color

Draw a picture of Jesus and you
and color

About the Author

Robert Schmidt was born to a professional country Western singer. His mother started teaching him to sing at age three, playing guitar and banjo by age five, and touring by age seven. Robert has devoted all of his music to Jesus. All of his music is now faith-based with scripture in the lyrics. He now continues to write, play, and record with his band Redeemed.